COMFORTING THOSE WHO GRIEVE

Comforting Those Who Grieve

A Guide for Helping Others

DOUG MANNING

1817

Harper & Row, Publishers, San Francisco

Cambridge, Hagerstown, New York, Philadelphia
London, Mexico City, São Paulo, Singapore, Sydney

To Tom and Etoile Manning
and to the memory of
J. M. and Betty Maddox—

parents and in-laws
whose every touch on my life
has been soft, and warm, and meaningful.

COMFORTING THOSE WHO GRIEVE: *A Guide for Helping Others.* Copyright © 1985 by
In-Sight Books, Inc. All rights reserved. Printed in the United States of America.
No part of this book may be used or reproduced in any manner whatsoever
without written permission except in the case of brief quotations embodied in
critical articles and reviews. For information address Harper & Row, Publishers,
Inc., 10 East 53rd Street, New York, NY 10022. Published simultaneously in
Canada by Fitzhenry & Whiteside, Limited, Toronto.

FIRST EDITION

Library of Congress Cataloging in Publication Data

Manning, Doug.
    COMFORTING THOSE WHO GRIEVE.

    1. Bereavement—Religious aspects—Christianity.
2. Consolation. 3. Funeral rites and ceremonies.
I. Title.
BV4905.2.M279   1985   248.8′6   84-48226
ISBN 0-06-065418-X

84 85 86 87 88 10 9 8 7 6 5 4 3 2 1

Contents

Preface

This book is not designed to be a "How-To" manual on funerals. Canned sermons sound canned. Canned funeral sermons sound even worse. Every minister must develop a style that fits his or her personality.

This book was not written to give the minister another job to do nor another burden of guilt to bear over how the job is done. Each of us has enough to do and already more than enough guilt.

This book was written to help us understand how people feel while they recover from their wounds. It was written to help us realize how much we help by simply being there. Finally, I hope it helps us understand that when we have done what we can, it is time for us to admit we have done our best, and then relax without worry or guilt.

This book began years ago when a couple I know, Jess and Ann Wade, lost a precious little girl. At that time, Ann said, "Don't take my grief away from me. I deserve it, and I am going to have it." Her words on that dark night inspired me to investigate the process of grief.

This investigation has been aided by each of the families I have walked with through its grief. Their losses have helped me to express my thoughts on grief.

I. WHAT DO YOU SAY TO THOSE WHO GRIEVE?

1. Why Is It Important to Allow Grief?

Grief is one of the major social problems of our time. It is not considered a social problem, but unresolved grief can be the cause of many ills that plague society. We normally regard grief as a period of sorrow that has very little long-range effects. However, many of the things we call social problems had their beginnings in grief or trauma that was never faced and, therefore, never resolved. The long-term effects of unresolved grief can be devastating.

Therapists almost always delve into the backgrounds of their clients, trying to find clues to explain the causes of the problem that brought the client to therapy. In a large majority of cases the problems can be linked to grief or trauma that has never been resolved. Grief can have this kind of long-lasting effect, and yet it is usually not considered a serious condition that needs any special attention. Most people are left to fend for themselves and work through grief as best they can.

Many divorces are the result of the damage done by unresolved grief. This can have a profound effect on the personality of a person, and it can determine to a great degree how well a person can adjust to life and remarriage.

We know that it is extremely hard for a marriage to survive the grief caused by the death of a child. The divorce rate among such couples is about 70 percent. The hurt forces them to live at a survival level, and when people are trying to survive, they are concerned with themselves to such a degree they cannot see the needs of others. Couples trying to survive tend to destroy their marriages. Coping with grief properly could have a positive effect on the rate of divorce.

Alcoholism, also, can stem from grief or trauma. Far too many people drink in an effort to mask the pain or to avoid facing the feelings caused by grief, and the result is often another addition to the list of alcoholics in our world.

We rarely see these problems as a result of grief because they are usually well hidden. The effects of grief go unnoticed. It can be compared to a bruise which shows up after the cause of the bruise has been long forgotten. We bump our leg on a chair or a car door. As soon as the hurt is gone, we promptly forget the incident. A few days later a bruise appears, and we cannot remember the cause. The results of grief work the same way. When trauma strikes, we have certain thoughts, certain feelings, and reactions to the event. Gradually, the thoughts, feelings, and reactions become separate from the event. We develop thought patterns or a way of feeling or a way of reacting and never know what caused them to happen. Over the years these patterns become part of our personality. When they are programmed and set, we see the results, or the bruise, and do not see the cause.

A friend of mine lost her husband in a farm accident. I wanted to help her through her grief process, so I gave her a little book I had written. The book was written for ministers, but I thought she could get something out of it. She had begun dating a fellow in another city and was getting interested in him even though he seemed to have many problems. Divorced for years, this man had a serious drinking problem, was chronically unemployed, and never opened up to anyone. My friend found out from his sister that he had lost two children fourteen years earlier. His response to their deaths was to clam up. He never mentioned the children to anyone in fourteen years, had never been to the cemetery, and had long ago put away their pictures. The subject was closed.

My friend insisted on reading a chapter from the book I had offered her. The chapter was titled, "Don't Take My Grief Away From Me." Her boyfriend did not want her to do so, but she was very persistent. Finally, at one in the morning he gave in and she read. At two he began to talk about the children. Sometime later he dug out their pictures from the bottom of his closet. At six the next morning they went to the cemetery.

His story is a classic example of grief being a social problem, or at least the cause of social problems. He had been an Olympic swimmer who never found the time to teach his children to swim. While visiting their grandparents, the kids decided to ride bareback on a horse. They rode the horse into a farm pond, fell off, and drowned. The father closed the door to all feelings. His method of dealing with grief was to not deal with grief. When the anger of grief came, it was directed toward his wife, and ultimately there was a divorce. When the feelings began to surface in spite of his efforts, he drank them into oblivion. Today he is a burned-out shell of a man. He has what we call social problems. Social problems hide behind unresolved grief.

A friend of mine has many irrational fears. It is almost as if he lives in fear that he might miss something to be fearful about. His world is one of misery. His greatest fear is that sooner or later he will be overwhelmed. Someday something will happen that he cannot handle, and he will not cope. He has tried about every cure imaginable in his search for peace. Too often, the cures dealt with the symptoms and not the disease. When my friend was fifteen years of age his father committed suicide in the backyard while my friend was in the house. No one helped the young man deal with his grief, his guilt, his anger, or his fear. The family reacted with a deep sense of shame. It was as if they had been tainted, and their reputations ruined, because the father had done the unthinkable. A darkness entered that young boy's life and has resulted in a grown man who lives in fear and waits for the final straw that he predicts will come to break his back and lead him to suicide.

Grief is a serious matter. It can have long-term effects on people. Since we ministers are concerned about the social problems in our world, we certainly should take a long look at grief as a cause of these problems. I find this exciting because it allows us to work in the area of prevention. I am tired of working on cures. I relish the thought of working in an area that might eliminate the cause of some divorces or some alcoholism before it begins.

2. What Is Expected of Those Who Want To Help?

Ministers get more criticism from people who are grieving than from anyone else. The criticism is often hidden behind veiled hints, and sometimes it is due to a martyr complex. However it comes, rest assured, we are often the targets.

I did not realize how prevalent this criticism was until I began to travel around the country speaking about grief. I thought I was the only minister being attacked by people who did not understand. I thought I was the only one to ever be criticized by the ones I helped the most. Since then I have found the problem to be universal.

Since I have written in the field, and since I do travel, I have the opportunity to hear from people who are grieving. They write or they seek me out when I am in their city. I have been amazed at how quickly they express their feelings about the shortcomings of their ministers in helping them with their grief.

A few weeks ago, a couple drove out to a retreat I was heading. They asked if they could drive me back to the airport. They had twin daughters, and one of the girls had committed suicide. I do not know of any hurt harder to take than the suicide of a child. This death seemed to be especially senseless. The girl was a college graduate, just getting started in life, and then she was gone. I was prepared to deal with this family and their grief. The first thing they wanted to talk about was the failure of their church and their pastor in helping them with their grief.

No one had said anything to them about their grief since the funeral. People were avoiding them. If they could not avoid them, they very carefully steered the conversation away from the death. No one would mention the name of their daughter. It were as though the rest of the world wanted the daughter forgotten forever.

I have been among groups and have heard the ministry as a whole come under attack. We say the wrong things. We say too much. We don't say enough. Recently, a man told of being so angry with his minister that he felt like striking him. The rest of the group agreed. I was stunned.

All ministers experience this type of criticism. Most of the time we hear about this criticism slowly in bits and pieces. A parishioner will hint that we need to visit a certain member, because "they are not doing well." The hidden suggestion may be that this member is telling the world how disapponted they are in the ministering they have received.

Witnessing the prevalence of this attitude has shocked me into trying to detect the cause of these negative feelings. I think most of the ill will comes from anger and false expectations.

There is anger in grief. Later in this book we will look at anger more completely, but for right now it is enough to say anger is always present in grief. This anger will be focused on something or someone. Often the anger is focused on the minister. It can also be focused on the physician, the funeral director, members of the family, or even on God. When it is focused on the minister, the criticism follows. It is not unusual for those who have been helped the most to be the ones whose anger is focused on the minister. In a clergy conference, a minister shared with us an experience of this nature. In spite of the time he spent and the comfort he gave, his parishioner was critical. In utter frustration he finally said, "What does this person want of me?" These experiences hurt.

One of the main purposes of this book is to help us understand the anger of grief. Understanding will not prevent it, but it can keep us from panicking when it does happen. It can help us not to judge ourselves too harshly, and it can prevent our going through the throes of guilt over something we cannot help.

We can also learn that people who are grieving are in transition. What they feel today is not what they will feel tomorrow. The anger will pass if they are not attacked and put on the defensive. Knowing this can help us deal with the anger and still allow for the possibility of a relationship when the storm is over.

One chapter in this book will deal with the practical ways we can dissipate a great deal of this anger and criticism. By "practical" I mean things we can do with the time we have. None of us have the time to minister to the degree we would like.

Recently, a seatmate on an airplane asked me where I was going. When I told her I was on my was to lead a seminar for ministers on the subject of grief, her response was, "Don't they know all about that?" This lady put her finger on one of the causes of criticism. People assume we are experts on almost everything. They expect us to be all things to all people. The truth is that most of us have had very little training related to the hurts of people. Most of the time we are left to our own devices in the area of grief. We go forth with very little equipment and do the best we can. The results don't always meet the expectations imposed upon us.

The study of grief can do much to help us meet these expectations. Even more important, it can help us see that we are not the key to resolving the grief of our people. Most of the help people receive while grieving must come from friends and relatives. The minister cannot do it all. Time alone determines this for us. Out of this study we can learn how to train people for this work, and we can also learn how to be comfortable doing our part and letting others do the rest.

After thirty years in the ministry I know the pressures of trying to live up to unrealistic expectations. If this book helps us deal with these pressures more effectively, it has done its job well.

3. Grief Defined

Grief is the natural response to any loss. We tend to think of grief resulting only in response to death. Any loss creates grief. Losing a billfold can cause a sense of emptiness. This grief is not as intense or long-lasting as the grief accompanying a death, but it is grief nonetheless.

Displacement brings grief. I was speaking about the process of grief to a social agency. One of the social workers observed that I was describing the pattern experienced by the refugees she was dealing with. They had lost home, family, and culture. The result of this loss was a feeling of grief. A minister's wife related how she broke down in a grocery store after a recent move to a new city. She thought the move had been made without adverse effect, and then suddenly it hit her. People who are moved into a nursing home go through grief. Often, the family does not recognize it and reacts with deep guilt while the grief persists.

Divorce can cause grief. People who go through a divorce also experience the same feeling of grief as those who lose a loved one through death. Those going through a divorce claim their grief is worse. They say at least death gives closure, while in divorce the person is still there and must be dealt with again and again.

Grief, then, is the natural response to any loss. The key word is that it is *natural.* There is an orderly process people go through in dealing with grief. This process is nature's way of healing a broken heart. There are no short cuts. There are no magic words nor magic cures. If a person breaks a leg, a cast is put on the leg, and the physician instructs that crutches be used to keep pressure off the leg for an extended period of time. No one suggests that the time be shortened or the crutches not be used. We give nature time to heal broken legs. Grief can mean a broken heart. It is the most painful blow a person can receive. When it strikes, the person must have permission to go through the process of healing.

Ann and Jess Wade, friends of mine from Tulsa, suffered the sudden death of a child. The child had the croup, the condition worsened, and the child was admitted to the hospital. The doctor saw nothing serious, put the child under oxygen, and sent Jess home to care for the other child. In thirty minutes the child was dead. Ann was hysterical. Everyone was trying to get her to calm down and "get hold of herself." She stopped suddenly and said some of the most profound words I have ever heard. She said, "Don't take my grief away from me. I deserve it, and I am going to have it." I was out of the city at the time. It is probably well that I was, for had I been there, I would have been one of those trying to take her grief away from her.

Her words changed my concept of grief and recovery. They caused me to realize that I did not help people walk through grief—instead I spent a great deal of time trying to take grief away from people. Until this experience, I spent my time filling the air with philosophic statements so the people would stop crying. My actions were designed to help me avoid dealing with feelings. Somehow I had the idea that sympathy was bad for people. I must have believed that if I sympathized, they would just wallow in self-pity. I must have missed the example of Jesus weeping at the tomb of a friend.

Somehow I overlooked the natural process of the grief experience. This process lasts about two years. Sometimes it lasts longer, sometimes it may be a little shorter—but two years is the average. This means grief lasts much longer than most people expect. Recently, a poll was taken asking people how long grief lasted. The average answer was forty-eight hours. In this two-year period there are peaks and valleys. There will be an intense peak at an anniversary, birthday, holiday, and most Sundays. For some reason there will usually be a peak just before the two-year mark.

It is important for us to know how long grief lasts and also to understand its peaks. If we do not know this, we may decide the people are weak or do not have much faith, or are wallowing in self-pity. If we know, we can assure them that they are not crazy and are on schedule. Often we will need to assure the family involved. They may decide the person is not doing well and needs someone to straighten him or her out. The minister is usually the one chosen for this task.

If we do not understand the process and the time span of grief, we can become a source of pressure for the people experiencing grief. They will feel a great deal of pressure from friends and family. They will feel the need to show how strong they are or how much faith they have. This pressure can lead them to act well before they are well. The result will be unresolved grief.

The pressure can lead them into "the feel bad because you feel bad" syndrome. This syndrome results when a person has thoughts or feelings they cannot accept. They think: "I should not think this or feel in this way. There is something wrong with me or I would not think or feel this way; therefore, there is something wrong with me." This syndrome snowballs until sheer panic sets in, and the result is a devastated person.

Grief is a two-year, natural process people go through in healing a broken heart. It must be given time, and it must be natural. It must also be done in a way that suits the individual.

4. Grief as a Process

As the natural process of grief progresses, a person goes through about four stages. I hesitate using the word *stages* because it connotes definite movements from one phase to another. These stages are not well-defined. People will vacillate between the stages. They can be in stage three in the morning and be back in stage two by afternoon. Often they can be in two stages simultaneously.

The number of stages is unimportant. Some writers list them as three stages, some as high as ten. The important thing is to recognize the presence of stages or phases in the grief process. People will not think, feel, or react in the same way as time passes and the process develops. Too often, other people panic and begin to pressure the griever to change how he or she feels.

There are four stages or phases in grief:

1. Shock. The mind will protect itself from losing control. One of the protective devices built into the mind is the ability to shut out reality. When confronted with grief, the mind goes into a period of shock. This period is a time of vague unreality. The person is sad, but the whole scene has an unreal quality about it. This period is like watching a sad movie. We cry, but there is the sense that soon the movie will be over and all will be well. Just this week, a mother who had lost a son in an accident said, "All I can feel is that he is off somewhere and will come home any minute now."

The shock stage lasts for about three weeks. The time

will vary depending on the person involved and the suddenness of the loss. Sudden death creates more shock than a lingering illness. Even after a lingering death, there is shock. Gradually the shock gives way to reality.

2. Reality. This is the hardest part of grief. The person wakes up in the middle of the night facing the awful reality that they will never see their loved one again. This is when they feel the most pain. Their chest hurts, they feel as if they cannot breathe, there is a deep feeling that they cannot go on, and a very real fear that they are about to break.

This is the period when they call friends in the middle of the night and cry uncontrollably. This is the time when their friends feel the most helpless in their efforts to aid them. Ministers may feel this helplessness to the greatest degree of all. We feel as if we must say something to make them feel better. We wrack our brains trying to find the right words. There are no right words. This pain must be walked through. We would give almost anything if we could make it all go away, but the pain is real and the stage is necessary. In this stage, people need to talk. It is hard for us to think we are being much help when all we do is listen, but listening is needed at this point.

If they talk and are heard, gradually this stage will pass, and the person will move into the reaction phase.

3. Reaction. The impetus which moves a person from the reality stage to the reaction stage is anger. They hit bottom and get angry. There is anger in grief, but it will not always be recognized as anger. Sometimes it will be called hurt, frustration, guilt, fear, or rejection. These all stem from anger and can be looked at under the same general terms.

If someone slaps me, I will feel anger. I may deny the

presence of anger and call it by a nicer word, but I feel anger. Grief is more than a mere slap. Grief is an almost lethal blow to the soul. It also produces anger.

The presence of anger is not a bad thing. It is one of the healing emotions in grief. The problem is not the presence of anger, but finding permission to be angry. A person tends to think there is something wrong with them when they feel anger. This leads to the "feel bad because you feel bad" syndrome. This syndrome occurs when we have thoughts or feelings we think we should not have. Then we tell ourselves there is something wrong with us or we would not think or feel these things. The conclusion is, therefore, that there is something wrong. This can snowball into panic. It is also difficult to get permission for the anger from those around the person in grief. Others seem to panic when the grieving person feels angry. They react, and the person must defend his position. When he begins to defend, the anger is intensified, and the "growth through grief" process stops. We must remember that grief means transition. When a person expresses anger, it does not mean they will always feel this way. We must fight the tendency to react to their anger. Let them be mad—it is part of the process.

The only problem with the anger is that it must be focused on something. The hope is for the anger to be focused in the right places.

Sometimes the anger will express itself in irrational ways. It is not unusual for a person to get angry at a mate for dying and leaving them. This seems irrational, since the mate usually had no way to avoid death, except in cases of suicide. It seems irrational, but it is not a bad place for the anger to be focused.

One of the sweetest ladies I know found her anger

being focused on her mate. The first Thanksgiving after her mate died, the children insisted on her joining them for Thanksgiving dinner. She was not ready for such a family gathering, but the children insisted. They could not bear the thought of their mother being alone on Thanksgiving. The lady went, and had a miserable time. After the meal, she took dishes to the kitchen. She forgot that the window over her daughter's sink looked out on the cemetery across the street. She suddenly screamed, "Why did you leave me like this, you So and So?" Her daughter was entering the kitchen with a handful of dishes. The shock of her mother's outburst caused her to drop the dishes on the floor. The grandchildren heard the outburst and began running through the house in a panic, saying, "Grandmother is in the kitchen cussing Grandpa because he died."

What they could not understand was that the anger caused by the grief had to be focused somewhere. In this case it was being focused on the one who had died. Since this is irrational, it may seem inappropriate. It is one of the more natural and even healthy places for anger to be focused.

Sometimes anger will focus on the minister, the funeral director, the physician, or on friends. When this happens, the person will talk at great length about how these people have failed them. In a recent conference, one person said, "The thing that made me mad was when people said, 'I know just how you feel.' They could not know how I felt." In the same conference another person said, "I got mad when they said I do not know how you feel, and I feel helpless." I thought, "Here I am hurting, and you are telling me your troubles."

Experiences like this make us wonder if there is anything to say. There really is no right thing to say, but the issue is not what is said. The issue is: There is anger in grief, and it must be focused somewhere. In cases like these I try to deal with the anger. I say, "You seem to be feeling a great deal of anger. You should feel anger. It is a natural result of grief." Then we talk about the anger, and not the slights.

Sometimes anger is focused on God. This is when ministers are the most likely to react. We feel we must defend God. Our reaction causes the person to defend their position. The more they defend the harder it is for them to get over their anger. God is big enough and loving enough to handle anger in his children. He does not need our defense. If we can fight the tendency to react, and deal with the presence of anger, those in grief can let down their defenses and grow, even through their anger with God.

The most dangerous place for anger to focus is inward. If the anger cannot be expressed toward an external source, then it will be turned inward, and people will be angry at themselves. They begin to be eaten up with self-incrimination. They begin to play the game of "if only." I sometimes think if there were no guilt in grief, we would create some.

I went to a home where a daughter-in-law had been murdered. The couple thought the husband was the one experiencing the most difficulty and that I could help him. He related his problem, with anger, toward the person who had committed the murder. He shared how he could gladly kill this person with his bare hands. The wife said, "Anger is not my problem. My problem is that I helped the kids find their apartment in the city where the murder took place. Now, if I had not found this apartment, the girl would not have been there. If she had not been there, the murderer would not have found her, and she would still be alive."

I said, "I am glad you are not angry."

She said, "What do you mean?"

I said, "Your are just as angry as your husband. You just do not feel free to be angry at the person who did the crime. So you are turning your anger inward and are mad at yourself."

When people begin the "if onlys," we must not argue with their logic. We must help them see the presence of anger and lead them to focus the anger on something besides themselves.

In the reaction stage, people will usually reveal various symtoms that let us know how they feel. Often these symptoms are frightening to us. Often the family will see the symptoms and decide the person is not handling his grief. The family can decide the person has stagnated and is now wallowing in self-pity. This is not true. The person is dealing with grief in his own way. The symptoms will pass. The symptoms will pass much more quickly if the person is not attacked and put on the defensive. Some of these symptoms are:

Sleep.   Some people try to avoid their pain by sleeping. They will talk about how much sleep they seem to need. "I sleep all night and still can't get enough. As soon as I get home, I sleep some more."

Activity.   Some people get very busy. They are afraid to stop. If they stop, they will think, so they get active. To avoid thinking they will clean the house, and then clean it again. They think they have a great burst of energy, but in reality, they are staying busy to avoid thinking.

Hyper-religious.   Some people turn to religion with a vengeance. They seek out every emotional religious experience possible. They will make elaborate promises to God. There is nothing wrong with this, but we need to realize that it, too, will pass—and the promises will be forgotten.

Drink. This is the most dangerous. They will pass through this stage, but there is the chance of addiction before the stage is passed. These people are trying to mask the hurt. We must help them see the problem without attacking the drink.

Promiscuousness. This one is hard to understand. It is more prevalent in the grief following divorce than in the grief following death, but it happens in both cases. Some people go through a stage of needing love so deeply that they turn to promiscuity to fill the need. One of the dangers is that they will marry far too soon because of the guilt they feel over their lifestyle. They need a careful hand and a great deal of understanding to work through their feelings. This, too, will pass.

The key in each of these symptoms is for us to deal with the disease and not the symptom. The disease is the pain of grief. If we attack the symptom, the person defends their position, and nothing is done about the disease.

4. Recovery. There is a final stage. People do recover and reconstruct their lives. However, they are never the same. They may be stronger and better people as a result of the experience, but there will always be a certain amount of scar tissue.

Most of the time people will know when they have recovered. There is a time when they decide to get well. Often this decision will be marked by the person being able to deal with something they have avoided until this time. It may be clothes they could not move from the house. It may be a chair they could not sit in. They all seem to have one area that can now be faced and conquered.

I told a friend that she would one day decide to get well, and when she did she would be able to deal with something she could not face now. She said it was the desk in her den. The desk contained all of the family pictures, and she could not bear to open it or clear out the pictures. She felt the day she could clear the desk she would know she was on her way. She called me to come to her house late one night. I went thinking there was some emergency. She stood by a clean desk with a smile on her face. She had decided to get well.

This decision can come suddenly. One lady said she was leaving church one morning. In the middle of the street it suddenly hit her that she had to decide whether to live or die. She decided to live.

At the end of a clergy conference I was leading, one minister told me he had planned to go by the home of a friend when the conference was over and confront his friends's wife. His friend had been dead about a year, and his wife still had her husband's golf clubs in the trunk of the car. This minister had decided to go tell the lady to get those golf clubs out of the trunk. After the conference he decided to wait until the lady was ready to deal with the golf clubs on her own. He said, "I don't know why I thought it to be my business whether or not those clubs were in the car." Funny how hard it is to wait for people to walk through the process of grief and decide in their own time to get well.

Grief is a process, a natural process. Our struggle as ministers is to allow people the freedom and the time to go through the process in the slow and natural method they need.

II. THE FUNERAL

5. Raising the Right Issues

After returning from a conference on funerals, I felt extremely frustrated. My frustration was like an itch in the middle of the back that you just can't reach. I sat through hours of issue-raising conferences while the issue I itched about was never raised. I heard a great deal about the cost of funerals. It was as if every funeral director in the world was a rip-off artist. I sat through hours of criticism of funeral practices and was reminded how pagan we are. I sat through ravings against flowers, open caskets, expensive vaults, and plastic services. Still, my itch was there.

I itched because I thought we were dealing with the wrong issues. There is one issue which overrides all those we belabored into boredom. That issue is: Do we help people get over grief? If so, the cost is such a minor consideration it is hardly worth mentioning. If not, then all the cost-cutting in the world will not help. We never did deal with the issue. So my itch did not go away. I determined to return home and deal with this issue in any form I could find.

Early in my ministry I was confronted with the storm raised by Jessica Mitford's book, *The American Way of Death*. The media joined the attack, and suddenly funeral directors everywhere were viewed as charlatans robbing widows and orphans. The whole basis then was the cost. No one ever questioned whether or not the process helped people in grief. If it cost money, it was bad. The more it cost, the worse it was.

My struggle, then, was based on a conflict between the book and my own experience. All during my ministry I had worked closely with funeral directors in all types of cities and in all types of situations. Some of these men were certainly more competent than others. Some of them performed more services. Some of them seemed to care more deeply. Competent and caring or not, they had all been good men. I could not believe any of them were charlatans. I decided the problem must be confined to some other part of the country. Confined or not, the men I worked with were under attack, and I felt helpless to defend them.

For some reason, I have always been friends with the funeral director in whatever city I happened to serve. As a young man, I would go and sit with a young mortician while he prepared bodies, just to be there as a friend. Even before this, one of my childhood friends had become a mortician, and our friendship continued throughout his schooling and into our adult lives.

I have been there when these men worked. I have been there when they cried while embalming a person who happened to be a close friend. I have been there when they tried to steel themselves to be professional when the family came.

I have made it a practice to stay close to a family in death. I usually go with them to the funeral home to see the body for the first time. I have often been with them during the casket selection and arrangement sessions. I have talked with hundreds of families after the event. Rarely, if ever, have I felt a family was oversold or over-pressured by these men.

Certainly, funerals are expensive. They are getting more expensive every day. This expense is often a hardship for the family. All of this I readily recognize. There are some things which must be said about this cost— things I feel justify our examination before making cost the sole issue.

It is a cost affected more by social pressure than by funeral salesmen. When selecting a service, a family is far more attuned to their own need for appearances, and far more attuned to their own feelings of guilt than they are to some sales pitch. Most of the time the funeral director is very carefully seeking to direct them to the service they can afford. It is of no advantage to him to sell something he cannot collect for. Through it all he must be a businessman. If he sells more than a family can pay for, he is only buying trouble for himself. I am sure there are those who do so. If they do, they will not last long in this field. Their bills are the hardest to collect of any bills I know. They cannot afford to sue and still live in the community. They can't afford to oversell, and in most cases they do not do so.

It is a cost we are helped to meet. Social Security, Veteran's benefits, insurance, and burial policies end up aiding in most cases. It is rare that a family does not have at least one of these aids. The cost is a blow, but it is a blow we are usually more prepared to meet than, for example, a car ruining an engine, or a fire, or any of the other major economic blows we might have to face.

It is a one-time cost. This may sound like an excuse but it is true, nonetheless. The funeral director has a high markup on his product. I doubt the markup is as high as is often reported, but it is high. It has to be. I do not want to sound crass, but the funeral director must make his total profit from one sale. The grocer can nibble away week by week and make 20 percent profit from us throughout our lives. The funeral director cannot do this. His business is one that must exist on a limited number of sales. In this respect, he is no different from certain other business men. The jeweler is a good example of a business man who must make his total profit on a limited number of sales. We do not buy a watch every week. Each customer represents a very limited number of watches in a lifetime. Whatever profit the jeweler is to receive from us, he must obtain in a very few sales. The fact is, all a funeral director is to receive from me he must make in this one event. It is an emotional event and, therefore, I may be super-sensitive about the profit. However, fairness demands his services be rewarded. I do not resent his receiving fair profit for being there when I need him the most.

The high cost of death is very real. If we are honest in our dealing with this high cost, we must look at more than the cost of the funeral. The funerals in my family have proven to be a minor part of the cost. The tax burden on estates can far exceed even the most elaborate funeral. The fee charged by attorneys for settling the estate should be examined in detail. It costs too much to die. A cheaper funeral will not lessen this cost to any great extent.

Now you can see why I itch. I get very tired of hearing the attack made against cost instead of service. To me the issue remains. Do these services help people get over grief? If so, the services are worth the price.

It seems to me that we as ministers need to take action on two fronts. First, we need to rise to the defense of funeral directors. The attack on them is surfacing once again. This time, we are included in the charge. The growing belief is that funerals are bad—period. The belief is that we, too, are not performing in this area, and that we are not necessary. I personally address my congregation, quite often, on the whole issue of funerals. I try to help them understand what is valuable and healthy and what is not of value and not healthy. I try to help them to pre-plan, so the decision is not made under emotional duress. All of this is part of an effort to help people face death.

We should also be sure people are being helped in facing grief. This may involve visiting with a funeral director and talking about areas of help. I have found these men most anxious to talk about grief and the methods for its healing. It may involve re-evaluating our own approach to the issue. I have worked hard in this area. To my amazement, I found I needed to restructure my approach. I also found I am being blessed by being more of a blessing. I am excited about some things I am now experiencing in the area of walking with people through grief.

May I share some of these things with you? I come not as an expert to tell you how to do your work. I come not as one who has arrived and is superior to you or even as one who has a better approach. I come as one interested in the field and anxious to share something I have found. I wish I could hear what you have found. Maybe we could help each other become better shepherds.

6. What Is Right About Funerals?

During the most effective funeral at which I ever officiated, I said almost nothing. I was called to hold a graveside service for the grandfather of a yound lady who was a counseling client of mine. I did not know the man, nor anyone else there, except the granddaughter. On the spur of the moment I simply told the assembled group that I did not know the man, but since they did, why not let them share their stories about who he was and what he meant to them.

Almost everyone had something to say. It was never a morbid scene in any sense. As a matter of fact, some of the time it was almost humorous. When everyone had finished, there was nothing left to say. The man had been memorialized to a degree I could never have matched. In the warmth of the moment, I closed in prayer.

The most dramatic funeral I can remember was an absolute celebration of the life, death, and hope of a friend of mine. His family were creative people with a flair for the dramatic. The celebration included slides and sound designed to go with the sermon in telling the story of his life. I worshiped that day, although I am sure most of the worshipers in the congregation were so shocked by the unusual service that worship may have been impossible.

The most unusual funeral I can remember was for the father of a friend of mine. At 1:30 in the afternoon we met at the cemetery for a private committal service. The family and a very few close friends were the only ones there. The service was a time of sharing with very few formal trappings. I felt it was a time of warmth for the family—a time of great meaning for them as they told their father good-bye.

At 2:30 there was a funeral service at the chapel. This was a memorial service done with great dignity and beauty. One of the aspects I noticed and enjoyed about this type of service was the unhurried atmosphere once it was over. We were not going to the cemetery, so we could all stand there and be warm to one another. We were not trying to get away from the cemetery, so we were in no way hurried or pushed or uncomfortable.

All of these different funerals made me feel good. I approached each of them with fear and trembling, for any change in the funeral can be disastrous. It seems to me very few people like funerals as they are, but no one has the courage to be the first one to do it differently. I have often heard people make long speeches against the current funeral practices, and then I have been with these same people when they prepared a very traditional service for a loved one.

The service of committal, separate from the funeral, may be the answer for the future. In the cities, it is getting harder to have a crowd for a daytime funeral. Businesses are not as lenient about letting people off to attend. No one would even think of having a funeral at night, so we continue to have memorial services with twenty-five scattered throughout the chapel.

It might become necessary to have a private committal service in the afternoon, followed by a memorial service in the evening. This would allow more people to attend, and would probably be easier on the family, and be more meaningful to them.

This could also cut the cost of funerals. The funeral director would not be responsible for the vehicle expense of a long processional to the cemetery. He would simply transport the body there and have the service ready when the family arrived. He would not even need eleborate funeral coaches, since there would be no processional.

There would be no charges for police escorts or flower cars. The greatest saving would be in manpower. One or two persons could handle the committal, and no more than three could handle the memorial service. Those who fuss about costs never realize that a great deal of the cost comes from the traditional things we do at funerals. If there have to be vehicles in procession, the funeral costs go up when the costs of cars and gas go up.

All of these changes must be approached with caution. We must be sure our efforts at improving are not, in reality, efforts to deny the fact of death. Some of the time, when people are expounding on all of the evils of current funeral practices, they are trying fo promote nice funerals which avoid facing the fact of death. Death denied is not going to make death go away, nor will it remove the grief.

One of the problems we face in working with grief is the intense effort made to avoid the fact of death. Hospitals often put the terminally ill as far from the nurses' station as possible. Their buzzers are the last ones answered. Some hospitals even have carts with hidden compartments so bodies can be removed secretly. All of this is done because people cannot face death: To them it means defeat.

This same tendency carries over into the funeral. To have a service with no body present and, of course, no body viewed, may sound modern and humane, but, in fact, it may be another way to avoid death. I have never left a service of this type without an empty feeling in my stomach. Something was missing—something was left undone. Somehow it all seemed cold and dry. We had avoided death and in the process avoided comfort and healing.

To me all of this says: There is a place for the traditional. I do not want to see all of these things pass. Sometimes tradition is an old friend you can count on and lean on. Some of the traditional things can help a great deal.

I sat in the waiting room of a funeral home holding the hands of a young woman and her daughter. The preparations for viewing were being completed, and we were to see the body of their husband and father. Yesterday, he was alive and with them. A car wreck meant today he was gone. Neither the wife nor the daughter thought they could bear seeing the body. They were torn between running away from the funeral home and walking into the viewing room. As gently as I could I urgd them to stay and face the viewing.

This may sound strange in light of all the talk we hear about how pagan we are, particularly when it comes to viewing bodies. Pagan or not, I was trying to get these two hurting people to hurt even more by viewing the body. That may sound cruel and pagan. In reality, it was healing and necessary.

We walked in together and faced the shock. We stayed awhile without talking much. They would mention how he looked or how his hair was not combed right. Mostly, they just stood in awe and were still. We sat down on a couch for a moment. The wife said, "It isn't real until you see the body, is it? It hurts to see him there, but until now

I could not fathom all of this being real. Now I know it is true, and I must face it."

Viewing the body is one of the healthiest things we do in funerals. This is the area most criticized by those who feel our funeral practices are pagan. The viewing provides closure. A young college student attached the word *closure* to this event. She told of refusing to see the body of her mother and trying to avoid dealing with the death. She thought she had handled the loss perfectly. Several months passed with her feeling she had handled her mother's death with little pain. As she walked across the stage to receive her diploma during her high school graduation, she saw her father alone in the audience. The death of her mother crashed in on her, and she broke down on the stage. She went on to explain that her grandmother had recently died. She viewed the body, and she said, "This gives me closure. I dealt with the reality of my grandmother's death and did not delay my grieving."

A funeral director friend of mine lost a son in a plane crash. My friend received a packet of ashes that once had been his son. He could not deal with the reality of the loss. He had fantasies that his son had escaped the crash and was wandering in the mountains near the crash site. He chartered planes to search for his son. The only way he could finally face reality was to go through the ashes and find the teeth so that dental records could be compared. He had to experience closure.

A similar tragedy occurs when bodies are never found or when the MIA's from Vietnam, for example, are never confirmed dead. We need closure.

It sounds good to say we want to remember them as they were. We do not want to remember them in a casket covered with makeup, looking plastic. It sounds good to say, but in practice viewing the body is the first step toward reality and healing.

This alone justifies the work and art of the mortician. I have seen them work all night to prepare a body that no one but the family was going to see. Some people may call that plastic and pagan. I call it a necessary tool in the healing process.

I even like flowers. I hear they are a waste, and the money should be spent in other ways. The healing process must have people in it. In grief, people need people. They do not have to say much, but they need to say they care. Flowers say it when people cannot say it in person. I remember being at my grandmother's funeral. She meant a great deal to me, and I was in deep grief. From out of my grief I began to look at the flowers. They said she was loved by many people. They said what I needed to hear. I will give to charity on my own—right then I needed to receive. I am glad each flower was there.

I lived with my grandmother part of my life and, therefore, had long talks with her about a number of things. One of the things she spoke about was the death of her husband. He died a young man in the 1920s, but she still carried the memories. Very often, she would say she wished she could have afforded a vault for her husband. Then she would fuss at herself and tell herself it did not matter, and that she was not right in her thinking on the subject.

I never told the family about our conversation, and when she died they did not know she wanted a vault for her husband. Since she had not put him in one, they assumed she did not want one for herself, so the arrangements were made, and I kept quiet about the matter.

Now, I am a fairly sane man who knows there is no

vault nor sealer casket that is going to do much to preserve the body. I am intelligent enough to know the body is just a hull designed to go back to the dust. I am not morbid about it, nor do I carry my concern to any extreme. I do wish we had put her in a vault, though. I do not know what the cost would have been in the twenties when my grandfather died. Nor do I know what the cost would have been in the fifties when grandmother died. I do know the peace of mind would have been worth the cost. I know it is silly, but silly or not, if it gives peace, it is worth it.

There are some new things under the sun, aren't there? New ideas in funerals. I wish there was a national magazine published to share with ministers the new and helpful in funerals. Maybe we could lead in the needed changes of tradition. If we do not lead, there will be no changes made. But while we are changing things so drastically, let's keep some of the traditions—some of them help.

7. The Funeral As an Affirmation of Life

I have come full circle in the area of funerals. It may sound as though I lost my zeal in the process, but I do not feel as if I have.

There was a time when funerals produced great frustration for me. On the one hand, I wanted to help the family. On the other hand, my evangelical background made me feel as if I should preach a sermon designed to convert the living. My instinct was to be a comforter to the family. My background was to be an evangelist in all situations; even funerals. I was torn between the two, and no matter which way I chose, I was uncomfortable.

Maybe it is growth, maybe it is lost zeal, but I finally decided the funeral was a time to comfort those in grief and celebrate the significance of a life. The funeral is not the time for preaching sermons. This is my own choice, of course. All ministers must make their choices as they see them. I am not at all sure my choice is the one others should make. Each of us should be comfortable with what is done. I do not think we can be comfortable while torn between the two areas of comfort or sermonizing.

Several things influenced my decision. One was my study of the life of Jesus Christ. Jesus did not feel he had to preach a sermon on every occasion. He must have decided who he was, and how he loved was a witness. I decided if I loved people and could show that love on these occasions of sorrow, I was bearing witness.

I am happy to say I think it works. I have formed deep relationships with people out of funeral experiences—relationships I was not forming through preaching at them, but relationships which have led to folks discovering God. They were first attracted by the spirit of love.

I am no expert on funerals. I probably do not do as good a job as others do, but I would like to share with you some of the things I do in a funeral to help people begin the recovery process.

The first and most important thing I do is during the private time with families. This will be discussed fully in the next chapter. For now, it is sufficient to say the process of recovery begins during these times.

The second thing I try to do is memorialize the person. I often hear pastors talk as if eulogies are in some way bad. To brag about the person somehow detracts from glorifying God. I do not believe this at all. The person matters to God. Did God not say every hair on a person's head was numbered? The person has a witness to bear for God. God is glorified by the work He has done in the life of the person. When I am talking about the life of the person, I feel I am glorifying God.

This matters because the family needs to feel the person was significant. I try to point out the significance, and I try to do so in as down-to-earth and human a way as possible. Recalling anecdotes, events, even humor, says this person mattered in our lives.

I have spoken about the importance of a mother. In the process I have tried to point out what it means to have a warm mother. How fortunate those who are so blessed.

I have spoken about the importance of humor in our world and the need for more men and women with humorous natures. "A merry heart doeth good like a medicine." (Prov. 17:22)

Of course, there are times when eulogies are difficult. Somehow I have always had the problem funerals. Murders, double murders, and suicides seem to search me out. Even in these deaths there is significance.

I remember officiating at the funeral of a young man who died in prison. He had spent more time in solitary confinement than any prisoner in the history of the state. Now he was dead, and only a few people were there to help his mother through the ordeal. I decided to face the issue head on. I said:

"It would be very easy for us to judge this life a failure and go our way. The trouble is we do not know the whole story. We only know the results. Who knows what fires burned within him? Who knows the hurts that were there? Who knows the causes? I have always felt that hurt people hurt people. God alone knows the whole story. He alone can pass judgment. We gather to say that He will pass judgment based on His knowledge of the whole story. This judgment will also be based on His infinite love of man. I am willing to leave judgments to Him and rest in the fact of His doing it in love."

I proceeded to try comforting the mother and then concluded the service. When it was over, I received the greatest compliment I ever received in my life. A businessman put his arm on my shoulder and said, "Preacher, you don't think there are any bad people, do you?"

I said, "No, I don't. There are some people who do bad things, but I don't know any bad people." I think this was an effective way to present the gospel by accident. If we reveal the love God has for all people then we have witnessed.

The third thing I do is try to give a sense of eternity. I deal with this theologically, of course, but I also deal with it in the human sense. I may say:

My Grandmother died almost twenty years ago. At least they said she was dead. In a real sense she is as alive today as she ever was. Hardly a day goes by but I think of Momma Hoyle. She still has deep meaning in my life. My children know her even though she died before they were born. They know her because every time the family gets together we swap yarns about her. We laugh at the funny and cry at the tragic. I not only know which stories will be told, I know the order in which they will come, for we always tell the same stories in the same order. I love these times of remembrance.

"Momma Hoyle dead? Not on your life. She cannot die as long as I am alive. She cannot die as long as my children are alive. We live on in the lives of those we love. This person, too, shall live on. Long after this day you will swap yarns and tell stories about the character he was. Your children will know him well. You never get over knowing someone like this. He is dead, and yet he lives—with God and with us.

The fourth thing I deal with is the issue of death. We have learned a great deal about death through the studies of those who have experienced death and been brought back. Most of us have read some of the marvelous books now available on the subject. I knew a lady who went through this experience. She gave me permission to tell her story, and I do so.

She was having a broken hip set, and without warning, she experienced cardiac arrest. They were able to bring her back, and she still lives. The next day I saw her in the hospital. She said, "Preacher, I am glad you are here. I don't know how to tell this. When I tell my family, they think I am crazy and want to die. I am 83 years old and do not have much to look forward to, but I am not morbid, nor do I want to die. When my heart stopped, I was outside my body looking back. I had the most wonderful feeling of well-being I have ever had in my life. I thought if I could just get them to get their hands off of me and let me go, everything would be all right. And Preacher, I fought them. I really did. I am ashamed of it, but I told them to get their hands off me. Now I feel like it was my trip, and they cheated me out of it."

I said, "I never thought I would ever say this to anyone, but I am sorry you did not get to make the trip."

She said, "Thank you. You understand."

Maybe this is what the Bible means when it says, "Death, where is thy sting?" Wouldn't it be just like God to make even death a pleasant experience! Wouldn't it be just like God to make death a passage into life! I think he made it just that.

What I am trying to do in funerals is give significance to life. I think God gets glory from life as he gave it to us, and life as he leads us to live it. In the process, I think families are helped in recovering from grief.

8. Private Time With the Family

The private sessions with the family grew out of my wanting the funeral to be a memorial to the person, and often I did not know the person. I began gathering the immediate family in a room, away from the crowd, to discuss the funeral. These sessions began to deal more and more with who the person was, and as a result, the sessions began to have more meaning to the family and to me.

I remembered the session our family had when my grandmother died. The night before the funeral, my father said, "Let's all go down and visit Momma Hoyle." We sat in the sleeproom where she lay in state, and we began to tell stories about who she was and what she meant. It was not a morbid event. We even laughed, at times, as we remembered the character she was. I do not remember ever shedding a tear that night, but I do remember the event with great fondness and emotion. I don't know what happened the next day at the funeral. The funeral, for me, was the night before with the family sharing stories.

I put the memory of this event together with the events that were taking place in bedrooms among other families, and I came up with the private funeral. I now ask the family to reserve a time the night before the funeral. I gather just the immediate family, somewhere away from the home where they are receiving callers. It can be at my office, or in the home of a close friend, or at the funeral home. The place does not matter as long as it provides freedom from interruption. We leave word at the home that the family is out for one hour and will return later. When I first mention this to a family, they are not sure about doing it. They are afraid the event will be morbid or overemotional. I assure them it will not be so, and they have always complied.

When we gather, I try to put them at ease and explain that a funeral should memorialize a person. I tell them I want them to help me know how to memorialize this person. I also say, "When I die I hope my family gets together to tell stories about me. I do not want this to be a sad event—I just want it to be a time of remembering."

At first, they will be reluctant to begin. Usually, a family will have a spokesperson who can easily be spotted. I simply ask that person to sum up the life of the person who has died. At first, the comments will be general in nature. For example:

"Well, Daddy was a good father."
"He was a kind person."
"Mother was the greatest mother in the whole world."

I simply keep them talking, and the conversation begins to move toward the personal. Someone will tell of a time when something was done or said. Another will remember the same event, and they are started. I rarely say very much else. Stories begin to tumble out: remembrances seem to surface. Some are funny, some serious, some emotional, but all of them are helpful.

These sessions will vary with each family. There is no way to predict how they will go nor which direction they will take. I have sat with families who had a great deal of bitterness within the group. These are the hard ones, but these are also the ones who need these sessions the most. They need to begin the process of facing their anger, and they need to find out they are not the only ones present with negative feelings. They rarely show much anger during the session, but they do not need to do so. If they can just say they have had problems with this person, they have taken a giant step. It is now in the open. They do not need to fake their way through the funeral or the living after the funeral. The most effective private funerals I have held have been these difficult ones. I leave feeling some people have been set free.

Other family sessions will be free of anger. During these sessions, the best thing that happens is the family drawing closer together. They begin to share each other's grief. Until this event they are consumed with their own grief. Now they begin to reach out to each other. It is easy to see the mutual healing that results.

Almost without exception, the family later tells me the private funeral was one of the best things they have ever experienced. I have heard that time and again. I did not know what it meant until my father-in-law died last summer.

There are two preachers in my wife's family. That is too many preachers for most families to handle, but in our case it has never been a problem. However, when the death occurred, neither myself or the other preacher wanted to take over, nor appear as though trying to direct the arrangements. As a result, I did not mention the private time. My wife and I were there for three or four days, but were never together alone. One of the problems families face in death is having to grieve in public. Friends are wonderful, and their presence means more than words can tell; however, it also means the family can never be alone. So we wandered around the house greeting people and making arrangements. We went through all the typical motions families go through in this experience—the days of gathering together, the funeral itself, and the business arrangements right after the funeral, before the children had to go home.

I drove home alone on the fourth day. This was the first time I could think through the event. It was also the first time I ever really grasped the importance of the private funeral. As I drove along, I was overwhelmed by all the things we did not say. I felt I would burst from the backlog of words I had not used. I had not told my mother-in-law what her husband had meant to me. I had not told my wife how much his passing hurt. I had not told the family how much I had gained from our relationship. I had not related the stories I now remembered and could not tell. There would never again be the same setting for all of these words to be expressed. We will be together at Christmas, but how could the subject even be brought up? The hurt of his passing was made worse by the hurt of words not spoken.

When my wife returned home we experienced a strange reluctance to approach the subject. I did not know how she felt, and was somehow afraid to tell her how I felt. It seemed as if I would be silly, or maybe I thought my hurt would make her hurt worse. For days we went about our living with no mention of her father. We hurt in silence, which is the worst hurt anyone can have.

Finally I could stand it no longer. I told my wife how I hurt. I told her of waking in the night with the awful emptiness of knowing I would never see him again. It

were as though a dam had been broken. She began to tell
of her hurt, and we were on our way to helping each
other in grief.

Through this experience I began to realize the poten-
tial of the private funeral. In thinking it through I decided
there were some basic needs a family has during this time.
It seems to me these basic needs can at least begin to be
met during such a private time as I described.

The family needs each other.   Just a private time to
be together helps more than I can say. I often leave the
private funeral and suggest that the family remain there
for a time. This may be the best time of all. There is no
one there except the ones they need the most, and a dialogue has already been started. My leaving often starts the
dialogue in earnest.

The family needs to share grief.   Until I know how
much you hurt, I do not feel comfortable telling you how
much I hurt. Unless there is a time for breaking down this
barrier, the family is likely to go on as if there were no
hurt. It may sound like this private time could lead to an
excess of sympathy and tears. It leads to just the opposite.
The family has now found freedom to speak about their
hurts. If they do not find this freedom, all they can do is
swallow feelings and put on a false front. One of the devastating things about grief is feeling that we must get over
it in a hurry, or else we are weak. This leads to faking
recovery. The results are disastrous mentally, physically,
and spiritually. People need freedom to hurt while they
hurt, and they need this freedom in their own family more
than anywhere else. Getting this freedom anywhere is
hard, but getting it in one's own family is hardest of all.
The private funeral gives this freedom where it counts the
most.

The family needs honesty. If there has been a problem among family members, it is either dealt with or it is destructive. Most depression is the result of swallowed anger. If the anger is toward a person, and that person is dead, there is no way to deal with it through confrontation. However, it can still be dealt with among the family. I do not mean someone should use this time to vent every hurt feeling. This has never happened in my experiences. I do mean a person can say, "As you know, Pop and I have had our difficulties. These have kept us from being real close, but I can see he had a side and I have a side. I am willing to let it rest there." Those are the exact words used in a recent private time. I thought they were significant.

The family needs a sense of significance. They told my father he had cancer. He told me he had often wondered what it would be like to be told this news. He said when they told him, his reaction was, "I have had a good life, because I have a lot of friends." Relationships are the ultimate things of value. When you come down to it, life means friends and family. When someone passes, it matters whether or not their life has had significance. It seems to soften the blow of death to know the value of the life.

During the private time, the family is dealing with this very thing. They are relating the significance of a life among the very people who were touched. I have left so many of these times feeling as if the family had suddenly discovered the true value of the life passed and the true value of their own life.

Just lately, I have been taking my funeral director friend along with me on these occasions. I do so because he is interested in the whole area of grief recovery, and also because he wants to learn how to direct one himself. I will not be around forever, and he intends to carry on after I am gone.

This is beautiful to me because it is the first step toward an ideal. The ideal is a preacher and a funeral director working together, helping people recover from grief. People need us both.

III. HOW TO HELP THOSE WHO GRIEVE

9. Being There

Most of the help people in grief receive comes from their friends. Unfortunately, most of the hurt they receive also comes from their friends. Any major effort at helping people walk through grief must focus on training people in the art of giving comfort.

Far too often it is assumed that the minister will give people all of the help and guidance they need during a time of bereavement. A minister might want to be the major source of comfort, but no matter how good his intentions might be, it is physically impossible. Lack of time, energy, and emotional strength will defeat any effort in this direction.

The best thing a minister can do for people in grief is to see that their friends are prepared to comfort them. This preparation can be made through sermons, special studies, seminars, books, and media presentations. The more we understand about grief and its processes, the better equipped we can be to do the work of a comforter. The Bible speaks of the comforter in rather lofty terms. Galatians 6:2 is one of many texts that give instructions like—"Bear one another's burdens and so fulfill the law of Christ." The work of comforting is universal in its scope. If we live long enough we will one day experience grief. Even while we are not experiencing grief, there is rarely a time when we do not know some friend who is in grief. Since comforting is a biblical concept and a universal need, it seems strange that we know so little about how it is to be done. A sermon on grief is quite rare. Seminars on the subject are relatively new. Our approach to grief and our approach to death have been to ignore them and hope they go away. The results are sometimes disastrous.

Everyone who goes through the hurt of grief will also know the pain caused by people saying the wrong things. They mean well and want to help, but have no idea what to say. They are uncomfortable and feel compelled to say something, so they try and in the process only add to the pain.

We seem to feel as if we must explain the event. The result is a lot of philosophical answers. These answers are usually designed to defend God, but do very little toward healing wounds.

A friend of mine lost a little girl. Someone told him that perhaps his little girl would have grown up to be a bad person, and God took her home before this could happen. This is comfort?

A seminary professor caught a young man asleep in the front row of his class. The professor stared at the young man until he awoke. Just as the student jerked awake, the professor asked, "Why is there evil and suffering in the world?"

The young man stammered, "I—I—I—well, I used to know the answer to that, but I forgot."

The professor turned to his class and said, "Mark this day well, for in the history of the world there have only been two people who have known the answer to this question. One was Jesus, and he did not tell us. The other was this young man, and he forgot it."

There are no philosophic answers available to explain the "why" of hurt and tragedy, yet somehow we feel compelled to try.

People need to understand their roles in times of grief. Our task is not to explain. Our task is to be there. All we have to do is just be there. We do not need to say anything at all. Our presence and a hug go farther than all of the explaining in the world.

A great deal of hurt comes from the pressure applied by friends. Most of them do not know how long grief lasts nor what stages it moves through. Most do not know that people in grief are in transition. How they feel today is just temporary. Tomorrow they will feel differently. Since the friends do not know all of this, they tend to panic. They begin to think the person in grief is not progressing fast enough. They do not understand the person's thoughts and feelings, and they decide the person needs straightening out. They begin to attack, and say things like: "Now it is time to put away the past," or "You just can't let yourself think or feel this way," or "Where is your faith?" As a result, the grieving person feels pressured and even attacked.

When people feel attacked, they feel compelled to defend. When they begin to defend their position, they tend to stop progressing through their grief. Long after they should have grown out of this grief they will still be defending their right to feel bad or angry. People who get mad at God and stay mad are almost always people who were attacked because of their anger with God. They defended their position and got stuck there.

One of the best things to say to people in grief is "Feel what you feel." This gives them freedom to be where they are and not feel the need to defend. If they can find freedom to be where they are, then they can move on. People in grief are in transition, but there must be freedom for them to be in transition.

A great deal of the hurt caused by friends comes from avoidance. It is a sad truth, but when a person loses a loved one he usually also loses friends. The friends feel uncomfortable because they do not know what to say, and they think they must say something. They do not know whether or not to mention the name of the one who is dead. They think they will reopen the wound if they do so. The one in grief wants to mention the name; they need to. They want the person to be remembered. Consequently, the tension of not knowing what to say and trying to avoid speaking the name creates a breach in the relationship.

Friends seem to have an inborn sense that sympathy is bad. They seem to have been programmed to think that if they sympathize, the person in grief will just get worse and wallow in self-pity. I do not know where this idea came from, but it seems to be almost universal.

The tensions created by all of this cause the friends to start avoiding the person in grief. They will make up excuses for a while, then to justify their excuses they will build resentment toward the person in grief. The avoiding leads to guilt. The longer they avoid, the harder it is to face the guilt. They will finally drop the person from their circle of friends.

A friend of mine and his wife knew three couples, all of whom were unusually close friends. After the death of this friend's son, the other couples began avoiding the bereft couple. Now the couples will cross the street to avoid even meeting my friend and his wife. The hurt of a son's death is made deeper by the loss of friends.

I have conducted some long-term seminars with people in grief. In every case, the one question these people want to ask but do not know how to is, "How am

I supposed to act?" They feel pressure to perform, but have no guidelines for the performance. For example, what is a widow? We need a new name for "widow." It sounds so harsh. How is a widow supposed to act? There are some unwritten rules we impose, but are they correct? One unwritten rule is that a widow is supposed to grieve for a year. What does this mean? Does it refer to dating? Is it always wrong for her to remarry before the year is up? Is she supposed to wear black? A widow is in a bind. If she grieves too long, she is weak and has no faith. If she does not grieve long enough, she did not love her husband. Who is to say what is long enough or too long? One lady said, "I would not buy a new car for two years. I could hear the people say, 'He is not even cold, and there she is out spending all of his money.'"

We have a long way to go in training people for dealing with grief. If they could understand the process, then they could relax and let their friends and families walk through it. If they could understand their role, then they could be comfortable with not always having an answer. If they could understand they are needed, they could assume responsibility without placing all the burden on the minister. If all this were accomplished, everyone would benefit and grief could be less painful.

10. Get Practical

There is no set pattern for ministering to those in grief. Each minister must design his or her own method. The method must fit the personality of the minister and be suited to the time allotted. We are people with different gifts and different callings. Some of us will be more comfortable with this type of ministry than others. Some will not excel in this area, but will have talent for other areas. The first and most important thing to consider is that we should work according to our gifts.

This does not excuse us from dealing with people in grief, but it should relieve us of guilt and pressure. We need to be free to minister in our own way. Some ministers will need to concentrate on training others. Some will need to delegate the responsibility to staff members. Some will enjoy the work and find it to be a natural part of their lives. It is not important how it is done or who does it. This book is trying to say what matters is that it be done. People in grief need help.

There are some practical things all of us can do—little things that mean a great deal—things that say we remember and care.

Books. There are some very fine books available which we can provide. I wrote *Don't Take My Grief Away,* because I felt the need for something to take with me when I called on a family after a death. The first call is always a hectic experience. There is a constant flow of people which makes conversation impossible. There is the need for funeral arrangements which takes up what little conversation there is. I have always felt these calls were inadequate and incomplete. I leave the book and have been surprised at how often it is read on that first night. There are many books of this nature on the market. I think it is a good idea for a minister to find the one that seems appropriate and take it with him on the first call. It is also a good idea for the minister to sign the book with a few personal words. At a later date, when the anger of grief may be focused on the minister, there is tangible evidence that someone cares.

Flowers. Many churches send flowers to a grieving family. Even though the family will receive more flowers than they can handle, the gesture still means a great deal. The idea of a contribution to a charity in lieu of flowers sounds good in theory. In practice it is rather cold and impersonal. If flowers are sent, the minister's name should be on the card, because it is important for the family to receive something personal from the minister.

Talk. People in grief seem to ask for a personal word from the minister. They wait for this word to be initiated by the minister, and not by them. It does not need to be elaborate. A simple "I am thinking about you" is often enough. The one thing they cannot stand is for the minister to avoid their grief. Everyone else is avoiding—they at least want the minister to face it. If we avoid, they feel we expect them to go on as if nothing has happened. This, more than any other feeling, brings their anger to focus on us.

In the first part of this book I told of the couple whose daughter committed suicide. Their anger was focused on the church and the ministers. Their major complaint was that everyone seemed to expect them to act as if it had not happened. No one said anything about their grief. Their conclusion was that no one cared. The first encounter after the funeral is crucial. The family is eager to know we have not forgotten their hurt.

Anniversaries. Any holiday or anniversary is especially hard on a person in grief. The first anniversary of a death is particularly painful. Nothing helps like being remembered. Once, I saw a woman I knew in a restaurant, and I remembered that the first anniversary of her husband's death was that very day. I simply said to her, "I know this is a tough time, and I am thinking of you." She told every friend she had that I had remembered. It would be a good idea to keep a calendar of the death anniversaries in the church. A simple note from the minister will not open up old wounds. It will say, "You matter and are loved."

Mention names. No one is dead until they are forgotten. We live on eternally with God, but we also live on in the memory of those we have touched. People in grief want to tell their story. I speak to quite a few of the Compassionate Friends Chapters around the country. This is a group of people who have lost children. I do not know how much help my speeches provide, but I do know that the best help I offer is after the speech when one by one they seek me out to tell me their story.

I spoke to a state convention of Compassionate Friends in Tulsa, Oklahoma. During the convention I was to be interviewed by a reporter from the *Tulsa World.* When I arrived at the interview room I found the reporter weeping. She said, "This is terrible. I did not want to come here. I knew it would be morbid. Then I walked in and saw a bulletin board with pictures of the children who have died and stories about how they died. I can't take it."

I said, "Have you noticed that you are the only one crying in this place?"

She said, "Yes, but so what?"

"The 'so what' is that their showing pictures of dead children is morbid to you, but not to them. They are saying, 'Remember my child—know the significance of the life, no matter how short. Don't forget.' These people are trying to tell their story. Let them tell it."

It sounds as if we will tear open old wounds when we say to a widow, "You know, I sure miss Charlie," or "I was thinking of Bill the other day." The widow may cry, but when we say those things we sing music to their ears. They want to talk about the person.

None of these practical suggestions are miracle cures. None will insure that the family will not focus their anger on the minister. They are just some practical ways of personalizing your concern. If your concern is personalized, the family will know you care and will feel your touch. It does not take a great deal of time to minister to those in grief. A few minutes will do if the family feels a personal touch from one who means so much to them. **Anything personal is practical.**

11. The Grief Seminar

If you have an hour and a half a week to spare, you can perform miracles. That's all the time it takes to have a grief seminar for those who have recently lost a loved one. At the present time I keep three of these in progress —one for older people who have experienced the death of a mate in the last year, one for younger people who have lost either a mate or a child, and one for those who have recently divorced.

It may seem strange to include divorce in a grief seminar, but people going through divorce have the same grief process to deal with as those going through loss by death. Divorce certainly has different feelings involved in the grieving, but it is grief just the same.

I have learned some things through trial and error about setting up these groups and dealing with them. In the process, I have had good groups where healing was easy to see. I have also had difficult groups when it seemed we were just shadowboxing with each other and living in our own misery. I cannot guarantee you will have a good group each time. I am not sure I have any formula for insuring a good group. Maybe my experience can help you become involved and avoid a few mistakes. One thing I do know—good groups or bad groups, I think the involvement has been one of the best things I have ever experienced. I am very happy to have been a part of each of them. I recommend the concept to you wholeheartedly.

Forming a Group

I have formed these groups in two ways. First, I advertise that a group or seminar will be starting on a certain date to meet for eight sessions. The sessions will be held once a week for one and a half hours. The advantage to this approach is that a group needs to be formed voluntarily. People need to decide for themselves whether or not they wish to attend such a seminar. The simple advertising allows this freedom.

The disadvantage is that advertising attracts such a diverse range of people with such widely varying needs that it becomes difficult to mesh them into a single group. One group I formed using this approach included three people who had lost a mate in the past few months, and were hurting desperately, and eight people who had lost their mates years ago. The eight people came just because they were lonely and wanted a place to go. They would have been happy if the group had turned into a bridge club. They had long ago walked through the grief process and did not want to go through it all again. Since there were eight of them and only three of the others, the eight dominated and controlled the group. The three soon dropped out.

There needs to be an organization to meet the needs of people like the eight I mentioned. I have tried to meet these needs through an active singles program with a strong social emphasis. This singles program attracts never-marrieds, divorced, and widows or widowers who have had the time to recover.

A grief seminar needs to be there for those who have experienced loss recently enough that they want to work on recovery. If each person in the group fits this description, the group can work together, aiming at this one need and seeking to discover methods of recovery.

The second method of organization is the one I now use. The people I know who are grieving are asked to join by personal invitation. Not all of these are members of my church. The funeral director helps me by mentioning names or even by contacting people for me. Usually, people in grief will find one another very soon after a death. This means almost everyone I ask will know one or two others who need to be in the group.

This does not guarantee a successful group, but it does mean they will all have the same set of needs. The groups formed in this way have proven to be more successful than the ones formed by advertising and accepting all who came.

Organizing the Group

At the first meeting it is necessary to agree on some simple guidelines. These are not so much rules as they are commitments the group members make to each other.

The first guideline is that no one will be forced to talk or reveal anything if they do not desire to do so. Most people enter a group with some fear that they will be "stripped naked" publicly. By expressing this guideline the tone is set for the group to relax.

The second guideline is that the group be closed. No one can join the group after it begins, unless the group as a whole discusses the idea and agrees. This is not done to be harsh in any way. It is done because a group cannot share if there is a constant influx of new people. To become a group is difficult. To get comfortable enough with any group of people to talk about feelings takes time and depends on becoming relaxed with the people there. Any addition of a new person to the group tends to stifle the flow for as long as it takes to get relaxed with the new person. It also takes several weeks for the new person to catch up to where the group is. Since I start a new group with regularity it is very easy to simply tell a new person they can join the next group when it begins.

The third guideline is confidentiality. We just do not talk to outside people about the things which are said in the group. This guideline is sometimes forgotten. When this happens I ask the person who has heard about the breach to bring it up in the group. Sometimes this is difficult. When it is dealt with in the open it can be a growing and healing experience.

The fourth guideline is attendance. A group must have continuity if it is to provide a sharing experience. If there is someone who attends only occasionally, they can stifle the group. I simply ask that they commit themselves to attend unless it is absolutely impossible for them to do so.

Any group will have dropouts. No matter how good the program, the leader, or the group, there will be some who are threatened by the experience. For this reason, if you wish your group to have eight people, you need to start with ten or twelve. Eight is the ideal number for the maximum size of a group. Anything larger is too big to become intimate. Fewer than eight is fine, and I have had great groups with as few as three. The problem is finding people who can relax and be comfortable in an experience of sharing.

At first I took the dropout rate personally. I felt as if I had said the wrong thing or had failed in some way. I now know this is the normal experience for any group. As soon as it becomes clear that feelings will be expressed some people are going to run. Often they return to later groups when they are ready for this kind of encounter.

Program

What do you say to people who are hurting? I imagine the fear of not knowing what to say is the major factor in keeping us from having programs to help them. It may be the major factor in our avoiding other contacts with these people. We seem to be afraid of saying the wrong things or of being caught with no answers to their questions. Programming, then, becomes a major problem.

This is a problem for which I have no simple solutions. The program should fit you and your personality. If you are comfortable with a nonstructured approach to things, then the program should be nonstructured. If you are comfortable with structure, then the program should be structured. Maybe we should look at both.

The nonstructured approach seems to fit my style better than any other. I simply call the group to order, make some opening comment that is designed to get the group talking, and let it flow from there. If they are comfortable with each other, I may not even make an opening comment. Usually, after three meetings, they are so anxious to talk I can't get a word in.

Some Suggestions for Opening Comments

First meeting. I open with a brief word about the guidelines of the group. Then I lead a dialogue about each person there which serves to get them acquainted with one another. I conclude by asking them what they hope to receive from the group.

Second meeting. The opening statement is about the

stages of grief, which leads to a discussion about each person's present status.

Third meeting. The opening statement is about anger as a stage of grief. This helps the group begin to talk about their own feelings of anger.

Fourth meeting. The opening statement is about the "feeling bad because you feel bad" syndrome that I discussed earlier. This is usually the best meeting so far. By now they are comfortable with each other and most people will be involved in the syndrome mentioned.

Fifth meeting. By this time I have learned a great deal from the group. I will usually begin this session with a statement about their progress as a group and as individuals.

Sixth meeting. I have learned that one of the major struggles is the search for appropriate behavior. How is a widow supposed to act? How long are they to mourn? What pressures do they feel? How do they think people see them? This leads to a discussion which touches a real nerve. No one has defined what is appropriate and, therefore, the widow is left in limbo. If she mourns too long, she is weak; if she does not mourn long enough, she did not love her mate.

Seventh meeting. I usually say nothing at all. I might just ask one person how he or she is doing and let things follow from there. If nothing happens, I might deal with financial matters or with the problem of sexual adjustment. Sometimes I start this session with the reactions to grief: sleep; drink; religious fervor; promiscuity. These reactions are covered briefly in chapter 4 of this book. The reason for discussing these reactions is to help assure people that they are normal. They are not the only ones who have reacted in such a manner. It also helps establish that these are stages and they, too, will pass. All this says is that by the seventh meeting we usually are progressing well enough not to need a beginning statement, but I keep these areas in mind because I want to deal with them at some stage if they have not already been covered.

Eighth meeting. I usually talk a few moments about purpose. What is the purpose of living? I try to lead them to see the purpose in their lives. I hope to convey the idea that there comes a time when they must decide to live again.

At the close of the eighth meeting we discuss whether or not to meet for a few more sessions. Usually we decide to do so, but at this time we also decide when the sessions will end.

The structured approach would be much the same but with more time for lecture, planned programs, films, and less time given to open discussion. There is much to be said for both methods. Use the method that fits you and your style.

The structured approach might include a book for group study. It is possible to use this book as a guide for such a study.

The structured approach might use the same outlines for meetings given for the unstructured. The talk period would be lengthened, and perhaps some definite questions prepared to use in the discussion period instead of open questioning with no control.

Difficult People

Every group will have some one person who seems to object to everything. Every suggestion will be met with forty reasons why it won't work. Every statement will be negative. What do you do with such people? Usually the group will handle it themseles. The time will come when they will confront the person, if they are a compatible group.

If not, I usually get the person alone and suggest some private sessions in addition to their participation in the group. The problem person is the one who needs the most help and is resisting the hardest. In private sessions I can usually help the person confront their situation realistically. The problem person can make the best progress if a breakthrough occurs. Most of the time they need to be confronted just as Jesus confronted the man at the pool. He said, "Do you want to get well?" For as much as they hurt, they may not want to get well, and have no idea that they do not want to do so.

Dissolving the Group

After the eighth meeting we may decide to continue for a few more sessions. At that time we also determine when the group will end. I do this for two very important reasons.

First: If there is a set cut-off date the group is aware the days are limited, and they must get down to business. If they have been holding back, they usually will let loose as the time draws to an end.

Second: There is danger in the group becoming too dependent on the leader. They may want to wallow in their grief and never get well. A group can only carry them so far—then it must become each person's struggle. The hardest part for the group may be the ending. You may feel as if you are leaving kittens by the side of the road, but hard or not, it is a necessary part of the healing process. The day must come when they decide to live again. That day can only come when they assume responsibility for themselves. It cannot come if they are overly dependent on a group or on the group leader.

It takes an hour and a half per week to do this. Nothing else I do gives me as much pleasure or does as much good as these experiences with grieving people. I may stop doing a lot of the things I do—I will never stop doing this work.

12. Listen

People in grief need someone to listen while they tell their story. Grief recovery requires the telling and retelling of their experience. In a sense people talk grief away. To those of us close to the grieving people, just listening does not seem to be enough help. We feel as if there should be more that we could do and should do.

I told a famous evangelist that I thought of myself as a divine healer. Since the evangelist is supposed to be a healer, I am sure he was not impressed. I went on to say that while he wanted to lay hands on people in order to heal them I wanted to lay ears on them. I think both ways, while different, are equally effective.

The ear is the most powerful part of the human body. We can do more with our ears than we can ever do with our tongues. I think I have "listened" more people into the Kingdom than I ever talked into it. One of the startling discoveries of my life was when I noticed how well-trained I was to talk and how untrained I was to listen.

Listening can make anger seem funny. Have you ever stewed in anger for a period of time and then finally told someone about the anger? While telling it, you could not make the event seem as bad as it was. Somehow the anger could not be sustained through the telling, and you finally just had to say, "I know it seems silly to you, and it probably is silly, but it made me angry." That is the power of listening taking the force out of anger.

Listening can ease worries. Try it the next time you

are worried. Fret for a day or so, and then tell someone about the worry. Almost inevitably the worry will begin to seem silly. You will end up saying, "Well, it seemed big at the time." That is the power of listening.

Listening can turn grief into growth. We do not take grief away from people—we simply help them walk through it. The method of walking through is to talk it out. They need to talk it out to a good listener.

If you want to heal people, learn to "lay ears" on them. People must solve their own problems. We cannot do it for them. We cannot work out their thinking or their feelings, because it is impossible for us to know what the person is really thinking or feeling in the depth of their souls. But we can give them the ingredient needed to work problems out for themselves, by listening while they talk.

Somehow, listening is hard. We feel we must say something. Not having an answer seems to say we are incompetent. People will put pressure on us to do so. They will even tell us we are not giving them an answer. When they say something like that, we tend to flinch inside and rush to the defense of our knowledge or lack of it.

If we can quietly sit there without reacting defensively when they apply this pressure, they will soon drop the pressure and let the talk flow. This takes great courage, but when it is done, the flow of their talk helps them sweep away the collected crud of their experiences.

People learn while they talk. They may be saying horrible things at the time, but while they are saying them their anger and frustration levels are shrinking. New insights are forming. After the storm there is a new peace.

I have used the power of listening to help the dying as well as the living. The first time I ever pulled a chair up to a bed and heard a person tell me they were going to die, I wanted to run. The urge to rush in with all sorts of assurances that they were not going to die was almost overwhelming. I braced myself and said, "Yes, it is certainly possible that you are—do you want to talk about it?" What followed was one of the great experiences of my life. I said very little, but a person worked through the fear of death as I listened.

The whole world is waiting to be heard. Off and on through the years I have taught a course on listening. In one course, there was a student who was very aloof. He was the last person I would expect people to go to with their troubles. He seemed cold and distant. During the course, he took the book we were studying to the research lab where he worked. He finally had to take the book home, so he could get his work done. It seemed people would notice the book and immediately begin to tell him their troubles. For this to happen to such a person means people are desperate for someone to listen to them.

This need is especially deep during grief. The ability to simply listen is the greatest help possible in every stage of grief. During the time of shock people need to tell the story again and again. As reality dawns, they need someone to explain it to. When reactions begin, they need someone who will accept the stage they are in.

The private funeral fits into this need beautifully. All the pastor is doing is providing a place for the personal and ears for the family. He not only hears them, he leads the family to hear one another.

A good listener becomes a walking, touching, personal, intensive care unit. That is what I want to be.